AFRICAN PROVERBS

WISDOM WITHOUT BORDERS

BY CLINT MORGAN

AFRICAN PROVERBS

WISDOM WITHOUT BORDERS

BY CLINT MORGAN

© 2015 by Clint Morgan

Published by Randall House Publications
114 Bush Road, Nashville, TN 37217

www.randallhouse.com

13-ISBN 9780892658725

Printed in the United States of America

KNOWLEDGE IS A GREAT POSSESSION BUT WISDOM IS A TRUE TREASURE.

Biblically I am convinced of this and from life's experience it is confirmed. The Bible very clearly instructs us to seek wisdom.

PROVERBS 1:5-6 (KJV)

A wise man will hear, and will increase learning; and a man of understanding shall attain unto wise counsels: To understand a proverb, and the interpretation; the words of the wise, and their dark sayings.

My wife and I spent nearly thirty years in Cote d'Ivoire, Africa. We became inculturated because we loved the people, the culture, and it was the logical course of action to ensure effective ministry and long-term survival. Although I no longer live there, never a day goes by that I do not think of Africa multiple times.

One thing I love deeply about Africa is the treasure of wisdom passed down from generation to generation through their fables and proverbs. They address real life issues in a non-confrontational, judicious manner that invites the listener to engage in discerning the lesson to be learned. I can't tell you how many times I found myself in a dilemma and an African brother dropped a proverb into his advice and left me to ponder the meaning. Many of those moments are locked permanently into my memory.

As you turn the pages of this book imagine yourself pondering a life issue. See in your mind an elderly African man or woman looking you squarely in the eye and with tender firmness offering you a nugget of wisdom that guides you to the answer of your life question.

IF THE HEAD IS AROUND, DON'T PUT THE HAT ON THE KNEE.

Do not usurp authority.

IF SOMEONE GIVES YOU
A CHICKEN, DON'T ASK
HOW MUCH IT WEIGHS.

Appreciate a gift
no matter how small it is.

NO MATTER HOW LONG A LOG LAYS IN THE WATER, IT WILL NOT BECOME A CROCODILE.

Sitting in church for years will not make a person a Christian.

PUT YOUR FAITH IN GOD, BUT TIE YOUR CAMEL TIGHT.

Partner common sense
with faith in God.

EVEN A BLIND MAN DOESN'T BURN HIS BEANS TWICE.

No solid excuse exists
for making the same
mistake twice.

YOU CAN'T LOOK IN A BOTTLE WITH BOTH EYES.

It is impossible to see
all aspects of a situation
all at once.

RAIN MAY BEAT DOWN ON THE LEOPARD, BUT IT CANNOT WASH OUT ITS SPOTS.

A person of great character
can withstand testing.

YOU CAN'T SPIT AND SWALLOW AT THE SAME TIME.

An angry person
will not be open to advice.

Take care when seeking to
destroy an enemy lest a
family member or friend
be inadvertently hurt
or destroyed.

I COME TO YOU WITH BOTH PALMS EXPOSED.

I am coming in peace...
with no weapons and
no hidden agenda.

A BEE DOESN'T START ITS HIVE WITH HONEY.

It takes hard work
to produce fruit.

WHEREVER THE SNAIL GOES, HE TAKES HIS SHELL WITH HIM.

We take our culture with us wherever we go. This does not give us the right to reject new cultures, but rather encourages us to be who we are in every environment.

THE TRUTH MAY MAKE YOUR EYES RED, BUT IT WILL NOT BREAK THE FRIENDSHIP.

Real friendship can withstand the test of truth.

THE NIGHT GIVES COUNSEL.

Sleep on a matter before making a decision.

YOU DON'T BUY A HORSE BY LOOKING AT ITS FOOTPRINTS.

Examine the whole plan before committing to it.

WE AREN'T WARMING
OURSELVES BY THE
SAME FIRE.

A difference of opinion exists.

NOTHING MAKES YOU THINK OF WATER LIKE A DROUGHT.

The greatest things in life are often taken for granted.

IF YOU SEE A LION SHOWING ITS TEETH, DON'T THINK IT IS SMILING.

Don't be deceived by leaders who speak with an apparent smile on their faces... their words may be destructive.

WAR HAS NO EYES.

Anger blinds us
to the damage
we may be doing.

CROSS THE RIVER
IN A CROWD AND
THE CROCODILE
WON'T EAT YOU.

Working together
provides protection
from the enemy.

BETWEEN TRUE FRIENDS EVEN WATER DRUNK TOGETHER IS SWEET.

Even the smallest things
are enjoyable when
shared with a friend.

NEVER BE Too
PooR To GIVE, NoR
Too RICH To RECEIVE.

Stay humble no matter what.

DO NOT LET WHAT YOU CANNOT DO, TEAR FROM YOUR HANDS WHAT YOU CAN.

Don't be so controlled by fear
that nothing is accomplished.

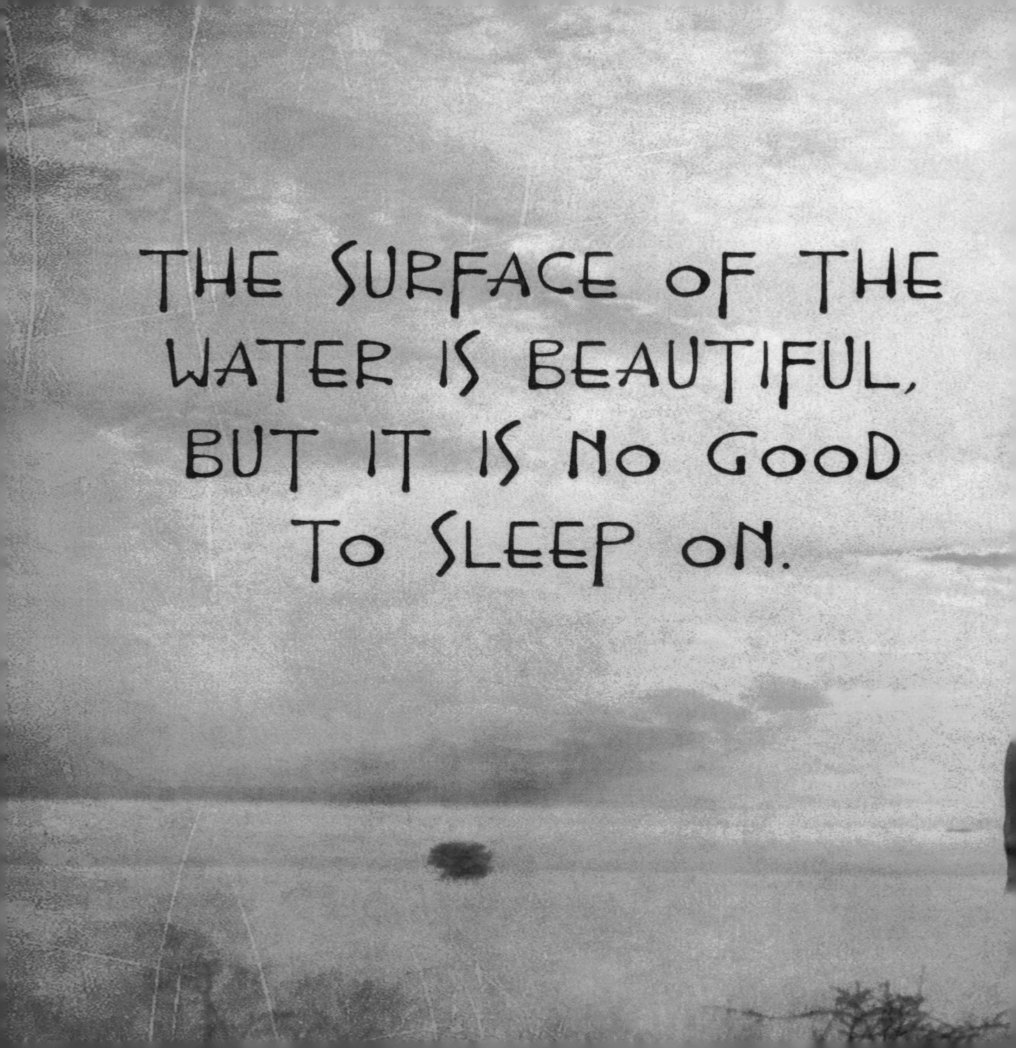

THE SURFACE OF THE
WATER IS BEAUTIFUL,
BUT IT IS NO GOOD
TO SLEEP ON.

Faith should be placed in what is solid,
not simply in what looks solid.

IF YOU THINK BEING SMALL ISN'T IMPORTANT, SPEND THE NIGHT WITH A MOSQUITO.

Never underestimate the possible destructive power of seemingly small mistakes.

THE AXE FORGETS, THE TREE REMEMBERS.

The offender forgets
what was done, but
the offended one
carries the scars
forever.

A FOOL HAS TO SAY SOMETHING; A WISE MAN HAS SOMETHING TO SAY.

The people who love to hear themselves talk generally have little to say. Listen to the words of the wise.

THE LION DOES NOT TURN AROUND WHEN A DOG BARKS.

A strong, confident leader
is not thrown off course
by small distractions.

WHEN THERE IS
NO ENEMY WITHIN,
THE ENEMIES OUTSIDE
CANNOT HURT YOU.

A peaceful heart provides
protection from the world.

IF YOU TELL A CHILD
NOT TO TOUCH
A HOT LAMP
HE MAY NOT LISTEN...
BUT, WHEN THE LAMP
TELLS HIM, HE WILL.

The consequences
of a bad decision
are more effective than
all the warnings given.

Meaningful, age-old words giving inspiration
and perspective fill this beautiful book.
Proverbs from another culture broaden our horizon
and pass along value, humor, and most of all
wisdom that truly stand the test of time.

Clint Morgan is the General Director of Free Will
Baptist International Missions. He and his wife Lynette
served with excellence as missionaries in Côte d'Ivoire
(1976-2005). The couple was involved in evangelism and
church planting before helping initiate and establish a
Bible institute for training Ivorian leaders. Clint was
instrumental in the development of The Hanna Project
in 2004, and was named its administrative director in
2010. The Morgans also served in France from 2007 to
2011. Clint and Lynette live in Nashville, Tennessee.
They have four children and six grandchildren.

randall house
114 Bush Rd. 1 Nashville, TN 37217
1-800-877-7030 1 randallhouse.com

RELIGION / Christian Life / Inspirational
ISBN 13: 978-0-89265-872-5

9 780892 658725